IMAGES OF ENGLAND

THE
BILLERICAY
SCHOOL

IMAGES OF ENGLAND

THE BILLERICAY SCHOOL

SYLVIA KENT

TEMPUS

Frontispiece: Billericay School received its third Schools Curriculum Award in April 1997. HRH The Princess Royal met students Louise Perry and Alex Storey. Also present were the former Chairman of Governors Peter Owen and Deputy Head Alan Vann.

First published 2003

Tempus Publishing Limited
The Mill, Brimscombe Port,
Stroud, Gloucestershire, GL5 2QG

British Library Cataloguing in Publication Data.
A catalogue record for this book is available from the British Library.

ISBN 0 7524 3083 1

Typesetting and origination by Tempus Publishing Limited
Printed in Great Britain by Midway Colour Print, Wiltshire

Contents

Acknowledgements

So many people have been generous with their time and in kindly allowing me to use their precious photographs and documents. Most of the information within this book has been given to me by contributors and accepted in good faith. I thank all those who appear in the following pages, including:

Mr Doug Brown, Mr and Mrs P. Bennett, Mrs Phyllis Burrows, Mr Stewart Clark, Mrs Betty Cranage, Mr David Cripps, Mrs Marion Davies, Mr Cyril Drake, Mr Don Drew, Mr Mike Edmonds, Mrs Betty Farrer, Mr Reg Ferriss, Mr Fred Fulcher, Mr Adam Henderson, Mrs Betty Howard, Mrs Charles Howard, Mr and Mrs John James, Mr and Mrs Keith Jillings, Mrs Florence Knowles, Mrs Ann Knowles, Mrs Hazel Martin, Mrs Jacqui Martin, Mr and Mrs Geoff Matthews, Mrs Doris May, Mr Ray Parmenter, Mrs Joan Pipe, Mr J. Reeve, Mr Neil Sansum, Mr and Mrs Lionel Scott, Mr Mike Shelley, Mr Jim Shrubb, Mrs Ann Simnett, Mr Lewis Smith, Mrs Mary Simpson, Mrs Mary Snowden, Mr Ewen Taylor, Mrs Heather Trotter, Mr David Watkins, Mrs Elsie Whale, Mr and Mrs Henry Whittaker, Mr and Mr Tony Whitworth, Mrs Eva Wood and Mrs Madeline Worrall.

Special thanks to Billericay School staff for their generous help, particularly Mrs Sue Hammond, Messrs John Walker, Alan Vann, Alan Sims, Ahson Mohammed, Alan Elkins, John Stevenson, Dr Roger Winter, Elaine Burford, Jacqui Clare and Margaret Turner.

For the use of press photographs, grateful thanks to Mr Martin McNeill, editor of the *Evening Echo*, and Mr Roger Watkins, editor of the *Billericay Gazette*; to photographers Mr Ron Poulter and Mr Peter Elgar; to Christine Brewster, curator of the Cater Museum, and special thanks to Mr Owen Bedwin at Essex County Council's Archaeological Department for permission to use material from the *Essex Archaeology and History Journal*.

Special thanks to: the Vice-Chairman of Governors, Mr Peter Owen, for his time and expert help; to Linda Elmy for her assistance; to Mr Arthur Lingard for his wonderful memories.

As always, love and appreciation to Peter, Sally and Jennifer for their patience over the past year.

A Brief History of Billericay School

A silver ceremonial key was used to open the doors of a new Billericay School in the last year of peace before the Second World War, unlocking a golden age of education in the town.

Since that day many thousands of young people have had good cause to be grateful for the education provided on a site where Bronze Age and Roman families once lived. It was Admiral Sir Vernon Haggard who used the silver key handed to him by Headteacher Mr P.G. White on 4 May 1938 to formally open the main doors of the building completed just a year earlier.

Under the contrasting leadership styles of a series of dedicated headteachers, Billericay School has remained at the forefront of new initiatives in education, accepting change and enhancing the opportunities it brings for the benefit of the students and the town it serves.

The school – today housing 1,750 students, 100 teachers and as many support staff – is in sharp contrast to its nineteenth-century forerunner, the Great Burstead Board School, which opened in 1878 just across the Laindon Road, for boys and girls between five and fourteen. Most children left by the age of twelve having reached the required Standard IV.

All this came in the wake of the Forster Education Act of 1870, the first government move to provide education for all the nation's children. The Great Burstead School Board was formed in the parish of which Billericay was just a part. Until then, apart from a small endowed grammar school opened here in the seventeenth century, the church and voluntary societies had run the only seats of learning.

The School Board was responsible for the organisation and finance of the school with occasional directives from the Department of Education – a far cry from today's welter of policy demands from Whitehall.

The first link in the chain of a series of successful heads came in 1923 with the appointment of Mr P.G. White, who, three years later, took over the newly formed Senior Mixed Department. By 1932 Billericay's population had grown to 3,690 and classes of fifty-eight were not uncommon. Plans were drawn up for its replacement on the seven-acre site that had impressive views out to the Thames estuary. David Marven, a contractor from Galleywood, built it under the direction of the county architect Mr J. Stuart for £22,400. The first children arrived in 1937, a year before the formal opening. Within two years, however, war clouds had gathered and distinctive new buildings appeared - air-raid shelters.

Some children were evacuated, but others recall that as the sirens sounded, children continued their lessons in the cramped shelters, chanting their tables and singing to drown the sounds of Luftwaffe bombers flying overhead en route to their London targets. Peace came, but within four years tragedy followed with the sudden death on holiday of Headteacher White, shortly before he was due to retire.

His successor, Ronald Eden, did much to encourage sport and Billericay School achieved success in football and cricket, along with hockey, tennis and netball. School trips began and also the first of many drama and musical productions.

In 1955 the popular John Goldwin arrived to take over the headship and the School Farm, which was to earn a unique reputation over the next forty years, was started under a series of dedicated teachers. The farm was to widen the scope of education in Billericay and broaden the knowledge of those students fortunate enough to share in it. It eventually fell victim to the pressures of the National Curriculum, squeezed out by more academic subjects.

Arthur Lingard came as headteacher in 1968, after successfully teaching at senior levels in grammar, modern and comprehensive schools. Mr Lingard piloted the school through its initiation into comprehensive education and beyond. He was determined to ensure that Billericay was not only one of the first large comprehensives in Essex, but the best. In an age when many of this contemporaries were publicity-shy. Mr Lingard opened the doors to the media at every opportunity to ensure that the school was also among the widely known. At least twelve of his appointed staff went on to headship locally and nationally.

All this happened against a backdrop of substantial rebuilding. The Sixth Form, created in the early 1960s, numbered just twenty-four when the school became comprehensive. Today there are ten times that number to be found in the superb new Sixth Form Centre.

In 1969, the house system was created with local historic names of Audley, Fitzwalter, de Vere and Christopher Martin. By 1972, when the school-leaving age was raised to sixteen, there were fifty teachers – half the present complement. A year earlier, the way was paved for today's large two-way involvement of students in international links with European countries. Exchanges began with French schools, and the annual trip to the Einstein Gymnasium in Reutlingen, Germany, continues thirty-two years on.

Arthur Lingard's educational vision and energy created a school that was popular with parents and students, not just because of excellence in examination results, but because the school's curriculum reflected the world students lived in. The Arts, Sport, Modern Languages, Science and Humanities blossomed beside the essential subjects of English and Mathematics. The school's reputation in Business and Technology led to it being invited to join national initiatives that pioneered vocational education in schools, and all students benefited from an influx of visiting experts who enthused students with both their knowledge and love of art, music, literature and drama.

During this time, the tremendous support that the school has received consistently from parents over the years was harnessed with the creation of the Parents Guild, later to be renamed Friends of Billericay School. Through their efforts, many thousands of

An early 1960s aerial view of the front of the school. Later, two houses in School Road were demolished to make way for the new school entrance and Roman Way.

pounds have been donated, making a real impact on the well-being of the students. Arthur Lingard retired in 1991 to be replaced by Robert Goodier, who took the school from management by the Local Education Authority to being self-governing and in doing so gained greater responsibility for its destiny.

Under the new grant-maintained system, the school employed its own teachers and support staff, and the maintenance and development of the grounds and premises became its responsibility. Inevitably this led to the school governors increasing their participation in the life of the school, ensuring that as the school moved forward it reflected the style and aspirations of the community it served. Sadly, ill health overtook Robert Goodier and in 1997 brought about his early retirement, but not before he, like his predecessors, had stamped his own style upon the evolving school.

The governors appointed Mrs Susan Hammond to be the school's first female headteacher. She brought with her tremendous energy, a great deal of experience born of tackling education in some of the more challenging areas of south-east London and Kent, and a management style that has earned respect from staff, pupils and parents.

She was soon to face the growing demands of bureaucracy that beset modern school life as tiers of administration have been passed from county level to schools. Mrs Hammond has ensured that the school still values those virtues that it believes lead to good citizenship. The golden age of education in Billericay, which began symbolically when that silver key was turned in 1938, is now entering a new and exciting phase.

From September 2003 the school becomes a Mathematics and Computing College. Welcome government money has arrived to underpin the new status, recognising the school as a centre of excellence in these subjects and taking on major curriculum development work that will benefit all students. The exciting new initiative ensures that doors are opened to adults and local businesses who may wish to gain or develop skills in these vital areas of learning. It brings a new impetus to the School Aims agreed in a mission statement by staff and governors several years ago:

> Giving individuals the opportunity to reach their potential in a caring and supportive environment that enables all members of the school community to succeed in a rapidly changing world.

The years ahead will undoubtedly be beset by change. New teachers and governors will stamp their unique mark on the school and new students will build on the reputation of those who, over the years, have gone on to highly successful careers born of their achievements at Billericay. The one constant remains: the school's desire to see happy and successful students leave its doors determined to make a caring contribution to the world they enter.

one

Early Education
in Billericay

Education in Billericay's agricultural community during the mid-nineteenth century was inadequate for children from working-class families. It is difficult to know what percentage of children from the labouring classes attended school; estimates suggest that it ranged from a third to a half in the decade following Queen Victoria's accession. There were free voluntary church schools by 1850 – the National Schools (Anglican) and the British Schools (Nonconformist) – but schoolrooms were small and overcrowded. Because many children were needed to help on the farms, particularly at harvest time, many could not attend school regularly.

Children from better-off families attended various private academies and 'dame schools' functioning from addresses in Billericay High Street. Among many proprietors of private schools listed in the local directories, John and Susannah Burningham were principals of a boarding and day academy, Mrs Moor ran a school at No. 49 High Street, Deborah Cross was head of a ladies' boarding academy and a Miss Houghton opened a tiny one-roomed school in Tanfield Drive.

Billericay once had its own endowed grammar school, founded in 1685 by Francis Bayly, Rector of North Benfleet. Its original site is unknown, but in 1863 its address was No. 94 High Street, later known as the Town Hall. This building was erected in 1830 as a market house and assembly rooms. The school shared the building with the local constabulary, and it had court rooms and cells at the rear. The playground was alongside. The grammar school closed in 1904, the last headteacher being Mr W. Mathews.

In 1848 the British School (Nonconformist) was founded in Chapel Street. Two hundred boys and girls were on register. One of its first headteachers was Mrs Sarah Hatch, whose husband was a gardener-seedsman in Billericay High Street.

On 25 March 1873, the School Board took over Rose Hall in Chapel Street and it became the Girls' School, pending the construction of the Great Burstead Board School in 1878. The Rose Hall still plays an important part in Billericay's community activities.

The boys attended the National Schoolroom in the Laindon Road, marked on the 1860 Great Burstead Ordnance Map. Built in 1839 of red brick, it was paid for by public subscription under the authority of Bishop Chapman. In 1873 this was taken over by the School Board and became the National Schoolroom for a few years before the Great Burstead Board School was built close by. This still stands today and is a meeting hall used by Billericay Scouts.

From 1860 to 1894, No. 117 High Street was the address of the Burstead House Academy. Described as a 'boarding school for gentlemen', its principal was Jonathan Henry Price. It was later known as Price's Academy. From 1910 to 1940, the building became the Burstead House Temperance Hotel. A garage was built on the site before the present supermarket.

Burstead House School for boys and girls stood at the north end of the High Street and was a distinctive landmark. Miss Annie Boughtwood was its principal for thirty years. The building was demolished in 1958 to make way for the major road development of Stock and Norsey Roads.

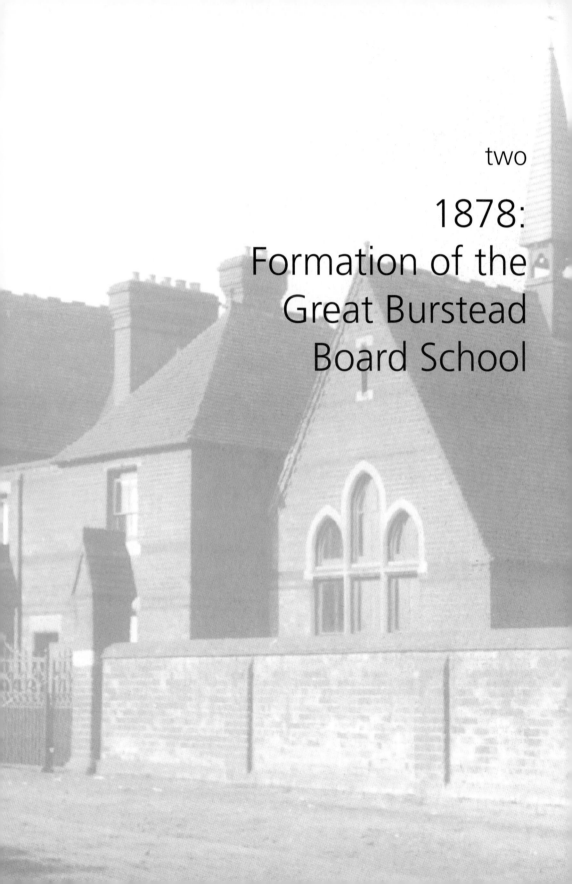

two

1878:
Formation of the
Great Burstead
Board School

The Great Burstead School Board was formed on 13 February 1873. Its introduction followed the celebrated Forster Act of 1870, which marked the first attempt by the government to provide education for all the nation's children. A search began to find a suitable piece of land on which to build a brand new school to accommodate the rising number of children in the parish. The ideal plot was found in the Laindon Road, not far from the National Boys' School (now the Scout Hut). It was purchased from the trustees of the late Thomas Richardson of Downham and measured one acre, two roods, nineteen perch and the price was £259. The money was loaned by the Public Works Loan Commissioners, with a repayment period of fifty years. A local architect, Mr Cutts, was chosen and the building work was carried out by Messrs Ruffell and Cross, both local men.

The cost of building the Great Burstead Board School was £4,897 10s and it was agreed that the building should be finished by 24 June 1878. Accommodation was provided for 400 children in two classrooms of 50ft by 18ft, with the boys on the north side, the girls on the south and the infants occupying a high gallery in the Girls' Department. In the centre, dividing the two, was the accommodation for the master and mistress respectively and a boardroom.

Major Thomas Spitty was the town's leading citizen during the eighteenth century. A wealthy landowner, he was an important influence in the establishment of the Great Burstead Board School and was chairman of the visitors. On 10 September 1878 Major Spitty formally opened the Great Burstead Board School's new premises. There was general celebration throughout the town. The children marched through the town and back to Mr Cole's meadow where Major Spitty had laid on a grand tea for the 338 children.

The journey to school along the Laindon Road often meant wet feet for some pupils who couldn't resist splashing in the weir pond as they passed by. During hard winters, skating was a popular pastime.

Quilters Farm stood at the junction with the Laindon and London Roads. Two Quilter girls, Florence and Daisy, attended Great Burstead School, became monitors, then teachers. May and Samuel, members of the Quilter family, also attended the local school in the early years of 1900. The family name lives on in the two schools built near the site in the early 1970s.

Opposite above: School records indicate that Mr Cornelius Smith and Mrs Hannah Cox were appointed master and mistress of the new schools. Mr Randall Porter became Head of the Boys' Department in the 1890s. Between 1899 and 1902, Mrs Clara Bushby became mistress of the Girls' Department, replacing her mother Mrs Hannah Cox. Education was not entirely free. Contributions varying from one penny to nine pence per week were expected from parents, depending on their status.

Opposite below: As Head of the Boys' Department at Great Burstead Board School, Mr Randall Porter served forty years. He appears in most of the early photographs taken. In this 1894 view, we see Mr Anderson, a young teacher, on the far right of the second row, and Jock Speller and Dick Scott in the back row. Percy Ross, Stan Cook, and Sam Crispin are in the second row and Len Galley is in the front row.

The windmill on the school badge is a reminder of the Billericay Post Mill that stood on Bell Hill for 200 years. It collapsed following a storm in November 1928.

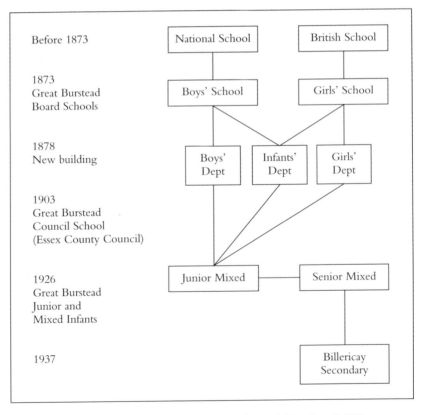

The origin and development of the Great Burstead Board School until 1937.

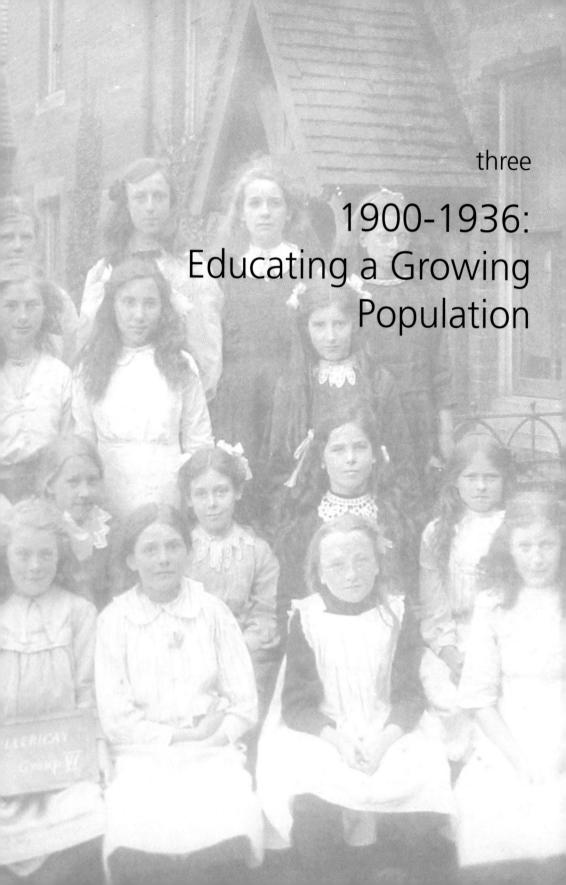

three

1900-1936: Educating a Growing Population

In this strongly agricultural area, working-class children were expected to work on the farms. By 1900, although the school leaving age was officially thirteen years, local bye-laws were applied so that children could leave school once they passed Standard IV. Pupils generally left Board School, having attained the three Rs in Standard IV at twelve years of age. By 1903 the County Councils had taken over all the public elementary schools, once the responsibility of the School Boards. They tried to maintain minimum standards and regular inspections were made by the authorities.

Football was of great importance at the Great Burstead School and many of the players in this 1905 view of the Billericay football team were former pupils. Back row, third from left: Richard (Dick) Scott; centre in bowler hat, Walter Totman; third from right, Sam Heard. Middle row, right: Sam Leeds; bottom right, Gillie Crook with brother Arthur on his right. Front row, left: Samuel Quilter.

Certificates for regular attendance were prized by pupils. William Barker, a pupil at Great Burstead School in 1908, was a proud owner of his good attendance certificate. In 1908, he and his brothers, Alfred and Arthur, boarded with Mrs Anstead, a local nurse, who fostered many children from East London in her small weir cottage in the Laindon Road.

Many local youngsters enjoyed taking part in the annual sports days, which were held on the football field at the side of the school. This 1908 view gives us a feel of the time. Note the Union flags welcoming the winner of this race. Sports prizes were displayed in a window of Fred Eales' saddlers' shop in the High Street to encourage participation in the events.

This 1911 photograph shows Group III girls, each one in their Sunday best. From left to right, back row: Gladys Edwards, Florrie Bond, Mary Balls, Dorothy Knightbridge, Doris Boughtwood. Middle row: Connie Speller, Hilda Arding, Doris Leeds, Jean Edwards, Gladys Little, -?- . Front row: Bessie Monk, Minnie Leeds, Vera Leeds, Elsie Thorogood, Bessie Harrington, ? Cowling.

A highlight of the annual Billericay Fête at the Great Burstead School was dancing around the maypole. This 1913 photograph from Mary Scott's album shows her mother, Kathleen Maryon (back row, third from left), her aunt, Jessie Wheeler (tenth from left), and girls from many old established Billericay families.

Right: This beautiful view of girls in the year before the First World War started seems timeless. Back row: Winifred Coppin, Dorothy Stammers, Winnie Westfield, Fanny Shergold. Second row: Ivy Andrews, Kathleen Maryon, Jessie Wheeler. Third row: Florrie Shipton, Maud Wheeler, Lily Stewart, Lily Knightbridge. Front row: Jean Shepherd, Winifred Caldwell, Jessie Tyler, Edith Bond.

Below: Gardening was on the timetable for the senior girls shown here in 1913. We know that Kathleen Maryon, Jessie Wheeler, Winifred and Mabel Coppin are part of the class, who were blissfully unaware that war would start the following year. Many of the pupils here are seen in the earlier photographs.

Above: This class of Group III girls in their Sunday best with intricate lace collars appear relaxed for the photographer. From left to right, back row: Lily Bright, -?- , May Emberson, Deeny Gay, Gladys Webber, -?- , ? Marshall, -?- , ? Watts. Third row: Lily Wright, Aggie Fell, Ivy Copsey, Marjorie Bassom, Evelyn Pearmain, Bessie Harrington, -?- , -?- , ? Cornell. Second row: -?- , -?- , Elsie Bond, -?- , Ivy Shipton, Eileen Copsey, Rosie Attridge, Ethel Gay. Front row: Nancy Mason, Elsie Coppin, Gladys Sewell, Evelyn Cridland, Ivy Speller.

Left: Elsie Whale (née Thorogood) became secretary to Mr P.G. White, headteacher of both the Great Burstead Junior and the Billericay Senior Schools.

The German Naval Airship Service Zeppelin L.32 in flight in 1915.

On 24 September 1916, Zeppelin L.32 was shot down over Billericay by twenty-three-year-old Second Lieutenant Frederick Sowrey. Several pupils at the school, including Elsie Thorogood (later Mrs Whale), were awakened by gunfire and witnessed the destruction of the Zeppelin. Soldiers are seen here guarding the burnt-out wreckage of the Zeppelin that crashed in a field off Green Farm Lane. The bodies of Oberleutnant zur See Werner Peterson, the commander, and his twenty-one-strong crew were buried at Great Burstead church, before being exhumed and buried at the German war cemetery in Cannock.

Grace Pearmain (later Mrs Bardwell) and Evelyn Pearmain (later Mrs Arthy) were pupils at the junior school during the First World War. Much is owed to Evelyn who later wrote her memoirs, detailing the day she and her sister rushed into Nix the High Street Chemist for shelter when an air raid took place at lunchtime. They were consoled by a bag of fruit drops given to them by Mr Nix.

This group of five-year-olds at the Great Burstead Board School poses happily in 1920. They include, from left to right, back row: Daisy Frost, Gladys Britton, Grace Geeves, Doris Stancombe, Florence Powell, Gladys Garland, -?- , Kathleen Worsell. Middle row: Peggy Plumb, -?- , -?- , Dulcie Mills, Ivy Hammond, Louise Watts. Front row: Helen Sillet, Melinda Ricketts, Ellen Smalley, Hilda Quarterman, Lily Stammers, Phyllis Hubbard.

Nine-year-old Phyllis Hubbard (now Mrs Burrows), second from right, enjoyed playing her role as a dragonfly in the *Mikado* in 1926.

Miss Dyer is remembered for her imaginative theatrical productions during the 1920s. The *Mikado*, performed in 1926, was a great success. Many of the performers still live locally.

Eva Wood (née Powell), back row, second from right, remembers the fun of being a member of the netball team of 1936.

Billericay's carnival was once a wonderful annual event, still remembered today. Jake Layland would lead the carnival procession along the High Street on his penny-farthing bicycle and people would make an effort to enter a float and dress up for the occasion. This superb float to carry 'Queen Elsie' was made by Horace Iles in 1936. Pupils from the Great Burstead School were encouraged to take part. Pupil Elsie Geeves was chosen to be queen that year and her attendants were all local girls. David Pearson was the page.

four

1937-1949:
Creation of the
Billericay Senior School

With an increasing population and burgeoning senior classes at Great Burstead School during the mid-1930s, work on the new large secondary school forged ahead. By September 1937, Headteacher Mr P.G. White and his staff were installed in the new school, and the senior classes with the autumn intake took the school roll to 375 pupils.

When war was declared in 1939, several teachers were called up to serve in the armed forces, as were former pupils, some of whom lost their lives. Air-raid shelters were built in the playground. Billericay residents became familiar with incendiary bombs, doodlebugs and during one night in 1940, the town narrowly missed being seriously damaged by a landmine. Luckily, Billericay escaped much of the bomb destruction experienced by neighbouring towns.

The land on which Billericay School was built was once a cornfield, remembered by older residents as being full of poppies every summer. A farm occupied the corner of School Road. The school, which occupied an acre, was built facing south. It was surrounded by six acres of playing fields. A century previous to this, a small iron foundry had existed near the site.

Mr D. Marven of Galleywood won the tender – amounting to £22,400 – to build the school under the supervision of Mr J. Stuart, the County Architect. The sand-faced bricks came from Mr Marven's brickyard on Galleywood Common and the sand-faced tiles were from Rettendon.

This old press cutting shows the splendid new school hall, opened officially in May 1938. The hall has been the centre not only for school assemblies, but for many community events, including performances of the Billericay Operatic Society. The hall still stands, but now serves as three classrooms in the old Block A. The original decorative plaster wall frieze still survives.

Above left: Cyril Drake, then an eleven-year-old, remembers his first day at the newly opened Billericay School. The sense of space after leaving his small junior school at Crays Hill made a great impression and he still remembers the evocative smell of new wood. The four houses in 1937 were Effingham (red), Raleigh (blue), Grenville (green), and Drake (yellow). The school motto 'Each for All', which was embroidered on the beehive crest, was designed by the headteacher's wife, Mrs Mabel White.

Above right: Cyril still keeps in touch with many of his former class-mates.

Mr White and his staff at the beginning of the September term, 1937. From left to right, back row: -?- , Mr Wilson Martin, Mr Pat Howard, Mr John Stokes, Mr Frank Martin, Mr Cliff Gardam, Mr Edwin Jones. Front row: -?- , Miss Harrison, Mr P.G. White, Miss Corcoran, Miss Linanne, Miss Bartlett.

Sheila Whitworth (née Webb) and some of her class-mates taking part in the 1937 carnival. This was an extra-special occasion as the new senior school had just opened and pupils enjoyed dressing up and representing their brand-new school. The lorry was supplied by Moys Coal. Also pictured are: Peter Owles, Sid Bridge, Phyllis Smith, Chrissie Halls, Mary Dodd, Derek Woodford, Daphne Mills, Queenie Woodley, Daphne Speller, Ronald Quarterman, Joan Collinson, Margaret Ager, Sheila Webb and Tony Whittaker.

Above: Another picture of youngsters from Billericay School taking part in the 1937 carnival. From left to right, back row: Sheila Webb, Margaret Ager, Joan Collinson. Middle row: Queenie Woodley, Phyllis Smith, Daphne Mills, Daphne Speller. Front row: -?- , -?- , Mary Dodd.

Right: The assembly hall provided a venue for many extra-curricula activities in Billericay. Here fourteen-year-old George Rix, one of a well-known family that attended Billericay School, shows off his sergeant's stripes as a member of the Army Cadet Force formed at the school during the Second World War.

Miss Harrison is remembered as being a popular teacher. She is pictured here in 1940 with her class. Sylvia Drake and Isobel Atkinson were new pupils at the school. The air-raid shelters were used frequently during this year. As soon as the air-raid sirens sounded, pupils headed for the shelters. They all carried their gas masks and a small emergency tin of food.

During the war years, film was almost unobtainable, so these photographs are treasured. Many of these pupils still live in Billericay. From left to right, back row: Heather Pheby, Joyce Benstead, Frank Harris, William Ball, Fred Bayliss, -?- , Tom Wilson. Middle row: -?- , Margaret Hodge, Joyce Weeden, Pam Butler, Joan Castell, -?- , -?- , Phyllis Matthews, Sheila Jeeves. Front row: -?- , -?- , -?- , Eric Hollingsworth, -?- .

Another picture, taken in the following year. From left to right, back row: Betty Brock, Pam Butler, -?- , Phyllis Matthews, Joyce Benstead, Ron Lee, -?- , Dulcie Jones, -?- , Joyce Weeden. Second row: George Sillett, -?- , -?- , -?- , -?- , Pat James, Arthur Hanbury, Frank Harris. Third row: -?- , Tom Wilson, Vic Cattaway, Frank Precious, Joyce Gimpson, -?- ,-?- , Joan Castell. Front row: -?- , -?- , -?- , Brenda Gimpson, William Ball.

A squadron of the Air Training Corps was formed at Billericay School as the Second World War began. Many of its members were pupils. Some of the older cadets went on to serve in the RAF. The roll of honour of Billericay cadets, most of whom attended the school, can still be seen at the Air Training Corps headquarters in Laindon Road.

Right: The Fulcher family were well known in Billericay. Brothers Fred and Jack both attended Billericay School. Jack, shown right, died in 1941 from a war accident and is fondly remembered by his brother, Fred, teachers and class-mates.

Below: Headteacher Mr P.G. White and his wife, Mabel, at the wedding of their daughter, Patricia, to Charles (Bill) Howard, brother of popular Maths teacher Mr Pat Howard.

LEAVING CERTIFICATE.

———::———

Name... Reginald - Rix ....

Age...14 years : 2 months.. Date of leaving..4·8·44...

Period at this School........3 years...............

Application.........A very reliable worker.

....

....

Best Subjects...General English and Maths...

GENERAL REMARKS.

......Reginald is a pleasant,.........
intelligent and well- mannered
lad, always keen on his work.

....

...............R.S.White...............Head Master.
                                           ~~Mistress.~~

Above: Miss Dorothy Strong was a favourite Home Economics teacher for many of the girls (boys opted for woodwork class). This photograph, believed to have been taken during 1941 shows classroom windows reinforced with tape as a prevention against bomb blast.

Left: School work continued throughout the war, despite regular air-raid warnings. Regular school reports were sent home at the end of each term. Reginald was one of eight Rix brothers to attend Billericay School.

1930-45

THEY DIED,
THAT WE MIGHT
LIVE

F.J. ALLEN	1st Essex Regt.
R. BASSOM	R.A.F.
K. BRIGHT	8th Royal Warwicks
S. BRIDGE	Irish Guards
C. DAVIES	R.A.F.
R.H. EVANS	R.N.
P. GURNETT	0th Herefords
H.T. JOEL	Glider Regt.
H. KENDALL	2nd Ryl West Kent
E. KEMP	R.A.C. 22nd Dragoons
P.G. KEMPEN	R.A.F.
R.A.KNOTT	Glider Regt.
S.J. MAY	R.N.
L. MAPES	2nd. Royal Norfolks
H.E. MITCHELL	R.A.F.
R. MOREL	R.A.F.
T. NEWTH	M.N.
D. PROUT	M.N.
F. READER	R.A.S.C.
L. ROBERTS	Rysal Corps of Signals
J. STEWART	5th. Essex Regt.
B. TIDMAN	R.A.F.
G.H. THIRKETTLE	R.A.F.
J.S. WALL	R.A.F.
D.A. WEBB	R.A.F.
E.W. WREN	1st. Essex Regt.
J.W. WATTS	1st. Dorset Regt.
J.E. VULCHER	R.A.F.
D.N. SHAW	R.A.F.

This war commemoration board in A Block lists the names of those who fell during the Second World War.

This 1946 picture of some of the Billericay senior girls shows them in their dancing costumes. They performed at other schools in the area. As material was in short supply, redundant blackout curtains were used to make the trousers. Pictured are: Josie Curtis, Janet Moore, Eileen Rawlings, Evelyn Quarterman, Evelyn Atkinson, Phyllis Taylor, Rita Howell, Joan Staines, Linda Bradley, Hazel Martin and June Willis.

Soon after the end of the Second World War, trips to France and Belgium were organised for the senior pupils, some of whom had to stay on one year as the school leaving age was raised to fifteen in 1947. Some pupils enjoyed the extra year, as this meant a chance to visit Paris for the first time. Jean Matthews (née Cayzer), back row centre, remembers her exciting Parisian trip and we see her here with class-mates outside their hotel. Miss Bowles, Mr Wilson Martin and Mr Pat Howard were in charge and Mr Clark, the Art teacher, organised the trip.

Mrs Marshall (far right) and staff in the assembly hall that served so many purposes, including feeding the pupils and staff. Her daughter, Betty, is seen here (also in white) with senior girls.

Above left: School dinners are remembered with mixed feelings, but this team of cooks headed by Mrs Marshall was excellent. Also pictured are Mrs Morgan, Mrs Cook and Mrs Cayzer.

Above right: This netball team of 1948 shows Madeline Tyler, Pauline Lammin, Maureen Carter, Janet Moore, ? Rowlands, Rosemary Moules and Linda Bradley proudly displaying the P.G. White Sports Shield.

Mr P.G. White and Mr Tony Whitworth, the PE teacher, with the football team of 1947. From left to right, back row: Peter Ball, Mr Tony Whitworth, Maurice Polley, Ronnie Newell, Donald Bull, Jimmy Nunn, -?- , Don Letch, Mr P.G. White. Front row: -?- , David Coupe, Maurice Elliott, Len Wren, Peter Stammers.

Staff members pictured in front of the school in 1948. From left to right, back row: Mr Tony Whitworth, Mr Joe Enever. Middle row: Mr Ken Collins, Mr Fred Rouse, Mr Eric Huggett, Mr Wilson Martin, Mr Pat Howard, Mr Ray Yardley, -?- . Front row: Miss Nora Glass, Miss Gwen Bowles, Mrs Mabel White, Mrs Urquhart, Mr P.G. White, Miss Norris, Miss Bartlett, Miss Linnane, Miss Killeen.

The football team of 1949, just after winning a match. From left to right, back row: Jimmy Wilkins, Mr Tony Whitworth, Tony Alston, -?- , Don Letch, Mr Ray Yardley, Mr P.G. White. Middle row: Len Wren, ? Polley. Front row: -?- , ? Coupe, Peter Storey, Len Atkinson, -?- , Peter Stammers.

Name......Owen Whittaker...........................

Term Ending...22nd July......., 1949. Class...2A....Year...2nd.

DETAILS OF THE REPORT.

SUBJECT	Marks Possible	Marks Obtained	REMARKS	Teacher's Signature
~~Holy Scripture~~ ...				
Arithmetic ...	20	14	Must work very hard	
Geometry ...	20	15	A very satisfactory year's work	
~~Algebra~~ Writing ...	20	19	Disappointing	S.B.
General English ...	20	18	V. Good	S.B.
English Literature ...	20	15½	Good	S.B.
English Composition ...	20	14	Promising	S.B.
Geography ...	20	17½	very satisfactory	
History ...	20	15	Good despite loss of time at extra choir practice	KCC
~~Science~~ Biology ...	20	17	Good - but note book not quite so careful lately	M.J.W
Handicraft ...	20	15	Good	
~~Needlework~~ ...				
~~Domestic Subjects~~ ...				
~~Hygiene~~ Reading ...	20	16	V. Good	
~~Home Nursing~~ ...				
~~First Aid~~ ...				
Music ...	20	13	Good	
Art ...	20	12	Fairly good	
Physical Exercises ...	20	9	Below average but Owen does his best & has a try at everything	
~~Shorthand~~ ...				
~~French~~ ...				
TOTALS	300	201		

FURTHER DETAILS.

No. in Class...28......   Position in Class...13/28.

Age of Scholar..13..yrs..8..mths.   Average age of Class..13..yrs..5..mths.

Conduct Marks lost.................   Conduct is......Excellent.

Attendance : ...16/38.......times absent, and......................times late.

General Remarks............................

Owen's pace is always "very gentle". A little more driving power would bring even better results

Next Term Begins ....5th September......1949.

(Signed)......S. Bartlett......Class Master. ~~Mistress.~~

......P. G. White......Head Master. ~~Mistress.~~

Declaration to be signed by Parent or Guardian of scholar.

I have duly considered the accompanying report of

......Owen Whittaker......

(Signed)......H. Whittaker......
(Parent ~~or Guardian.~~)

NOTICE :—The Head Teacher will be pleased to interview parents or guardians by appointment.

Above: A typical end of year report.

Left: Shortly before he was due to retire, Mr P.G. White died unexpectedly during the summer holidays in Cornwall, aged sixty.

five

1950-1967:
The Expanding Years

At the start of the 1950s, austerity was still widespread. Rationing of food and other products was continuing to cause hardship to parents and pupils alike. Following the death of Mr White in September 1949, the new headteacher, Mr Ronald Eden, joined the school. Links with the Great Burstead Junior and Mixed Infants (which became the Billericay Primary School in 1957 and, much later, was renamed Quilters) were still strong. Mr Eden was a keen sportsman. Cricket and football teams were particularly successful during the early 1950s. The 1944 Education Act triggered major changes in education and one of the effects nationally was the introduction of O-Level examinations in 1951. Register lists were growing and demountable classrooms were added to accommodate extra pupils. A Parents Guild was formed and one of their first projects was to build an open-air swimming pool.

Pictured in front of the school in autumn 1950 are, from left to right, back row: Mr Ray Yardley, Ron Baines, Tony Smalley, J. Reynolds, J. Coupe, Mr Ronald Eden. Middle row: Michael Shelley, Derek Burt, Norman Jones, Philip Hartshorn, Fred Ridgewell. Front row: Don Gilbert, Don Letch, Tony Manning.

This line-up of netball players, taken in 1950, includes, from back left: Marie Jeeves, Ann Marven, Kitty Adams, Wendy Speller, Phyllis Wright, Beryl Grimyard and Audrey Latter.

Miss Norris taught Music during the 1950s, but was also senior mistress. In this sports day picture she is pictured with head boy Vince Hawkings and proud recipient of the P.G. White Memorial Cup, Maureen Nash.

The former assembly hall in A Block was used for every occasion from school dinners to sport and music. This group of older pupils is performing a dance routine to the *Dambusters* tune. On the far right is Wendy Speller.

Sport was high on the agenda during 1950. From left to right, back row: Victor Plume, Ken Springett, -?- , Alec Jackson, -?- , David Coggins, Fred Gear, Leslie Bligh, Richard English, -?- . Middle row: -?- , -?- , -?- , -?- , -?- , Eric Payne, Jeremy Dauncy, Richard Bayment, Peter Cook, Henry Whittaker. Front row: Raymond Brock, David Cripps, -?- , Barrie Elliott, Leonard Atkinson, Derek Fairweather, Michael Staines, L. Travers, -?- .

Sports days usually meant speeches and on this special day Headteacher Mr Eden brought the school microphone out onto the field. Parents, pupils and teachers are in the crowd, including Ken Springett (third in the front row), head boy at the time.

Many members of Billericay families still living in the town are shown in this mixed PE group from around 1950. Among the group are, from left to right, back row: Alec Jackson, Ken Springett, Phyllis Taylor. Third row: Dick Fairweather, Michael Staines, Carol Taylor, Shirley Garrard. Second row: Terry King, Brian Dennington. Front row: David Cripps.

Under the guidance of their form teacher Mr Wilson Martin, the 3B boys embarked on producing a small book entitled *Yesterday, Today and Tomorrow*. Richard Bayment remembers this particular part of his schooldays: 'The form comprised thirty boys, average age fourteen, covering a wide range of aptitude, ability and interest. From a number of given topics, they themselves chose the book, debated titles, discussed subject matter and allocated themselves to the various tasks involved. Indeed, a verbatim report of those debates and discussions would occupy several volumes'.

The local Girl Guide company met weekly at Billericay School. Many of these guides also attended Billericay School. Guide Captain here was Mrs Turmeau. Wendy Speller is front row, second from the right.

Billericay School's hockey team was one of the best in the area. This early 1950s view shows Barbara Norton and Pam Bennett with their team.

The 1951 cricket team, with a splendid background of the school. From left to right, back row: ? Smith, Vic Brasted, J. Reynolds, Deric Burt, John Coupe, Lesley Kidgell. Front row: Ron Tony Smalley, Ron Baines, Michael Shelley, Mr Littlejohn, Mr Eden, Norman Jones, E. Garland, Tony Manning.

During the summer of 1950, Form 2A presented this production of *The Enchanted Shirt*. Among the actors are Norman Jones, Michael Shelley, Adam Henderson, ? Dudley, Fred Ridgewell and Leslie Kidgell. The beehive on the front of the proscenium was designed by Mrs Mabel White in 1937. It was gold–couched embroidery on a red velvet background.

BILLERICAY SECONDARY SCHOOL

THE SCHOLARS present

1066 AND ALL THAT

A Musical Comedy
By Reginald Arkell and Alfred Reynolds

At The School, School Road, Billericay
On FRIDAY, 16th MARCH, 1951, at 7.30

2/6 (Children Half Price)

Over half a century has passed since the Seniors put on the production *1066 And All That*, but former staff and pupils still remember the success of this musical comedy based on the Sellar and Yeatman script. Performed on the nights of 16 and 17 March 1951, there was standing room only for both evenings.

The whole cast of *1066 And All That* at the finale. Produced by Eric Huggett and Ken Collins, the wardrobe mistress was Miss Killeen, the stage manager was Walter Walkey, with Miss Norris on the piano, Fred Fulcher on the drums and other members of the teaching staff taking on supporting roles. With eighteen scenes and practically everyone in the school taking part, either on stage, providing the music or working back stage and doing props, this mammoth production must have taken months to rehearse. Henry Whittaker remembers helping to make the Roman soldiers' costumes. For this special occasion, the ingenious Mr Clark, Art teacher, designed and made the new school crest on the proscenium.

Frank Martin taught History and Geography for many years. Possessing a wonderful tenor voice, Mr Martin was one of the earliest members of the Billericay Operatic Society, founded in 1929.

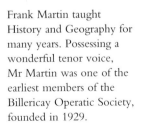

The Festival of Britain in 1951 caused great excitement nationally. Mr Wilson Martin is seen here with a group of older pupils at London's South Bank, resting on the steps of the famous Skylon.

The old quad was a favourite place when it came to taking photographs and here we see Headteacher Ronald Eden, flanked by Miss Norris, Mr Walter Walkey and prefects, at the end of summer 1952. Mr Walkey later went to live in Australia, but he kept in touch with many of his former pupils and fellow teachers.

Mr Wilson Martin taking a Science class during the mid-1950s. Peter Tilsey is present among the scholars.

Billericay School was the venue for many local organisations and societies. At one time, pupils who were members of the local British Red Cross Society, met regularly under the supervision of Mr Ken Simpson. The Area Commandant was Mrs King (back row, fourth from left). Avril and Victor Hardy are present in this photograph taken in the early 1950s.

Two bike sheds were built when the school was erected in 1937. Bicycles were essential, for many of the pupils lived in outlying villages and often there was no other form of transport. This was before some areas had a school bus service. Among the pupils here are John Tudor and Maurice Turner.

Many pupils who attended the senior school during 1953 will surely recognise their fellow class-mates in this carefree group of performers. Miss Ward organised this country dance group. The girls wore green gingham dresses. Those pictured include: Peter Snell, Sheila Keeling, Jean Rayner, Larry Lamb, Ann Coggins, Ian Wright, Ann Lucas, Trevor Nightingale, Ray Nunn, Elaine Carter, Bob Ireland, Carol Brown, Henry Graves, John McKenna, Billy Hughes, Ken Hutchings, Vic Hardy, Pam Quelch, Jean Reading, Mike Mortlock, Connie Crush, and Linda and Wendy Barker.

A fast game of netball shows Valerie Brown as goal attack. In the background stand the school's air-raid shelters, which were used by caretaking staff as storage sheds until the 1970s.

Miss Florence Powell (later Mrs Knowles) was a popular teacher at Great Burstead Junior School. She was an enthusiastic leader of the youth musical group that met in the evening at Billericay School during the mid-1950s. Miss Powell is centre right. Included in the gathering are: Sylvia Weeden, Margaret Colman, Ken Mills, Pat Howard, Brian Bright, Mildred Cordell, Frank Owen, Brian Nash, Arthur Spark, Jean Taylor, Michael Nash and Doreen Jackson.

A contemporary photograph of Mrs Florence Knowles (née Powell). Born in 1915, Mrs Knowles was a pupil at the Great Burstead School and remembers being taught by Miss Daisy Quilter. In 1927, Mrs Knowles won a scholarship to Brentwood County High School the year it opened. After receiving her teacher-training diploma at Goldsmiths College, she returned to teach at the Great Burstead Junior School until her early retirement in the late 1960s.

Prizegiving during the late 1950s. Mrs Monica Garton, then Head of the Girls' School, Jacqueline Stubberfield and Terry Kidgell with the County Education Officer.

The annual prizegiving at the end of term brought parents, governors and the town's leading citizens into school. From the left we see Mr J. Taylor, Mrs Gunter, Mr Albert Phelps, Reverend Holley, Headteacher Mr John Goldwin (appointed in 1955) and other members of the governing body.

The sack race, along with three-legged races and the egg-and-spoon race, was fun and provided a humorous side to sports day.

Who remembers trying to scale the buck or climb the wall bars? This posed picture in the assembly hall will bring back many dreadful memories for those who loathed PE. The subject was compulsory unless you brought a note!

Prizewinners of 1959. Among the students present are Roger Webster, Terence Reed, Richard Talbot, Alan Rice, Tony Smith and Nicholas Wheatley. With Headteacher Mr Goldwin are Miss Killeen, Mr Elias, Mr Brown, Miss Alford, Mrs Kefford, Mrs Hope, Mr Legg, Mr Ellis and Mr Butler.

This evening social event with Headteacher John Goldwin and Freda Staines (second left, front row) was organised by the Parents Guild. At the end of the 1950s, the private swimming club that was once part of Lake Meadows ceased operating, and £400 and six club trophies were presented to John Goldwin to assist the new swimming pool project.

A typical woodwork class during the 1950s.

During the 1950s, part of the curriculum included dressmaking classes, organised by Needlework teacher Mrs Urquhart. Pictured are Maureen Adams, Pamela Young and Rosemary Collier.

Mr Reg Ferriss, now governor of Billericay School and president of the Air Training Corps, taught Science there from 1953 to 1957. From left to right, back row: Mr Morris, Mr Walter Walkey, Mr Rouse, Mr Pat Howard, Mr Eric Huggett, Mr Wilson, Mr Ray Yardley, Mr Reg Ferriss. Front row: -?- Mrs Urquhart, Miss Killeen, Miss Norris, Mr Ronald Eden, -?- , -?- , -?- , -?- .

This 1956 photograph shows Mr Reg Ferris and his class, which included some of the youngsters from the Hutton Poplars Residential School. The following year, Mr Ferris left Billericay to take up his appointment at Sweyne Grammar School in Rayleigh.

Mr Eric Huggett taught at Billericay School for many years. He also ran the Scouts and put on many gang show performances, in the style of the then popular Ralph Reader. With good musical ability and a fine voice, he was an excellent pianist and a stalwart of the Billericay Operatic Society. In the group are: Richard Talbot, Peter Harris, Tony Fay, David Watkins, ? Jackson, John Drake, Ivor James, Dave Byers, Alan Keane, Broderick Lea and John Cooper.

Mr Clark is remembered as being an exceptionally gifted Art teacher during the 1950s. He also taught typing on huge black Imperial typewriters and today many of his former students are grateful for his early training as they zip along their computer keyboards. Here we see David Brown ignoring the photographer, intent on finishing his piece of sculpture.

Many pupils at the Senior School will remember their teachers from Billericay Junior School (later Quilters) just over the road. This 1954 photograph will bring back many memories. From left to right, back row: Mrs Grace Arthy, Mrs Molly Purdy, Mrs Polley, Mrs Myra Gay, Mrs Betty Farrer, Mrs Sylvia Williams. Front row: Mrs Wills, Mrs Ellen Williams, Mrs Norah Barry (headteacher), Mrs O'Dowd, Mrs Dorothy Tristram, Mrs Judy Rumsby.

This 1956 school line-up shows John Goldwin, who became headteacher in September 1955. Monica Garton became Head of the Girls' Department.

Sports day usually brought parents to cheer on and support their children. Guests were governors, the Reverend Smith and his wife Dorothea (front row, centre). The school grounds were extensive in the days before the redevelopment of the school a decade later.

Jim Childs, seen here in A Block corridor, was the caretaker in the 1950s, and he and his team kept the school clean and tidy.

With the help of the Parents Guild, the pool was built in the late 1950s. Here we see Charlie Cowling, Ron Lomond and Bill Thomas (far right) who, after retiring as school caretaker at the junior and senior schools, died in 1992, aged 101.

Right: The 1958/59 netball team. From left to right, back row: Brenda Rogers, Freda Staines, Jean Chalmers. Front row: Thelma Staines, Christine Pestell, Ann Furnell.

Below: A year later, Billericay School still had a strong team of netball players. From left to right, back row: Elaine Crook, Marlene Capon, Janet Keeling, -?- , -?- . Front row: -?- , Janet Aldous, Jill Smith, Wendy Foskett.

Mrs Monica Garton was Head of the Girls' Department when this photograph was taken at the end of the 1950s. This group includes Shirley Garrod, Phyllis Taylor, Ethel Brignall and Eileen Wilson, some of whom still live in Billericay.

1960 sports day. From left to right, back row: Pauline Randall, John Backburn, John Bright, Chris Knight. Second row: Eileen North, Catherine Smith, Jacqui Fell, Pamela Storey, Veronica Howard, Sandra Millard, Jennifer ?, Valerie Barber. Front row: Annette Dormer, Pam Adams, Janice Lilley, Rae Drury, Lyn Sallows.

Mr Hewitt (back row, centre) accompanied his class on a trip to Norwich and the Norfolk Broads at the end of the 1950s. In view are Martin Higgins, Roland Jackson, Andrew Roberts, Peter Cater, Mike Edmonds, Roy Hardwick, Michael Aldous, Phil Lees, Ivor Little, Elizabeth Bright, Kenneth Keil, Michael Carey, Brian Adams, Jeff Savill, Chris Terry, Bobby De'Ath, Daphne Polley, Elaine Denham, Jennifer Stubberfield and Stan Brockies.

The actor and entertainer Mike Edmonds (also seen in the previous photograph) enjoyed his time at Billericay School and keeps in touch with former class-mates. He began his acting career in the theatre which later led to fifteen films, including *Star Wars* and *Time Bandits*. As well as appearing in film, theatre and pantomime, Mike travels extensively, appearing in many television commercials made in overseas locations. He is seen in the above right photograph on the far left.

This picture, taken in 1961, shows Mr Ince, Miss Killeen, Miss Alford and many of the kitchen and Domestic Science staff, along with the Senior Girls.

Music has always been a vital part of Billericay School curriculum. In this 1961 photograph, we see Mr Stan Hewitt with his musicians during a Christmas performance.

Students studying commercial subjects visited the fiftieth National Business Efficiency Exhibition in the Grand Hall at Olympia. Miss Alford and Mr Brown accompanied the students.

The summer would not have been the same without the annual school trip to Clacton from Southend during the early 1960s. Many remember the *Medway Queen*. In view are Mr John Goldwin, Mr Walter Walkey, Mr Pat Howard and Mr Butler, with other members of staff and pupils from the senior classes, including Jim Sturley, Patrick Spall, Michael Timmis and Willy Harris. They returned home by coach.

This early 1960s group of pupils and teachers is ready to board the Channel Airways flight to Eze sur Mer in France. Miss Killeen, Mr Goldwin and Mr Parfitt organised the trip and pictured are David Watkins, Wayne Boughen, Geraldine Osborne, David Collins, Pearl Duff, Robin Pipe, Roger Kidd, David Collins, Terry Matthews, Rae Drury, John Drake, Dave Tilsley and Lewis Smith (back row, far right).

This early 1960s photograph shows pupils at morning assembly. Dark green blazers and grey trousers for boys were the uniform of the day. The badge depicted the windmill as it does today, but then it was green and yellow.

This 1963 line-up features Headteacher Mr Goldwin (centre), flanked by Mr Leonard Rosslyn and Mrs Monica Garton, plus many other teachers of the era. The four school houses had by this time changed to Stockwell, Norsey, Blunts and Chantry.

A vintage 1963 end-of-term line-up of prefects with Mr Leonard Rosslyn. From left to right, back row: Roy Allan, Terry Matthews, Ivor James. Third row: George Pincent, David Watkins, David Catherall, Keith Ransom, Anthony Jones, Len Hill, George Babb. Second row: Ann Mallen, Richard Talbot, -?- , Harry Barham, Graham Simmons, Bob Angel, Gloria Shayler, Bridget Townes. Front row: Elaine Dennis, Miriam Horrex, Linda Cain, Mr Rosslyn, Carol Wilcox, Eileen Mulvenna, -?- , Linda Turner.

Prizegiving day in the school hall, *c.* 1964, showing Marion Wood (now Davies) and Miriam Horrex (now Reed) with class-mates.

In 1965, after twenty-eight years serving as school secretary to Headteacher Mr P.G. White at Great Burstead Junior School, and for a time at Billericay Senior School, Mrs Elsie Whale (centre) retired.

A sports day photograph in 1966. From left to right, back row: Sally Munro, Ann Thorogood, -?- , Pamela Cain. Front row: -?- , Marion Wood, Gillian Redfern.

Class 5E end-of-term line-up in 1966. From left to right, back row: Stuart Williams, Stephen Dunkley, Christopher Cannon, Edward Taylor, Richard Wilson. Middle row: Christopher Perkins, Christopher Bouett, Rowena Prickett, Valerie Monk, Ann Cole, Jane Goldwin, Barbara Reed, Catherine Beckwith, Catherine Purdy. Front row: Sally Munro, Frances Goss, Pamela Cain, Marion Wood, Shelley Talbot.

The 1966 Christmas concert performed for older Billericay residents was part of the Sixth Form Community Care programme. Those involved include Christopher Cannon, Jane Goldwin, Shelley Talbot, Marion Wood, Lorraine Fletcher and Ann Cole.

A line-up of enthusiastic competitors at the 1967 County Sports Basildon District Team Sports event includes Marion Wood, Shelley Talbot, Brenda Owen and Gillian Redfern.

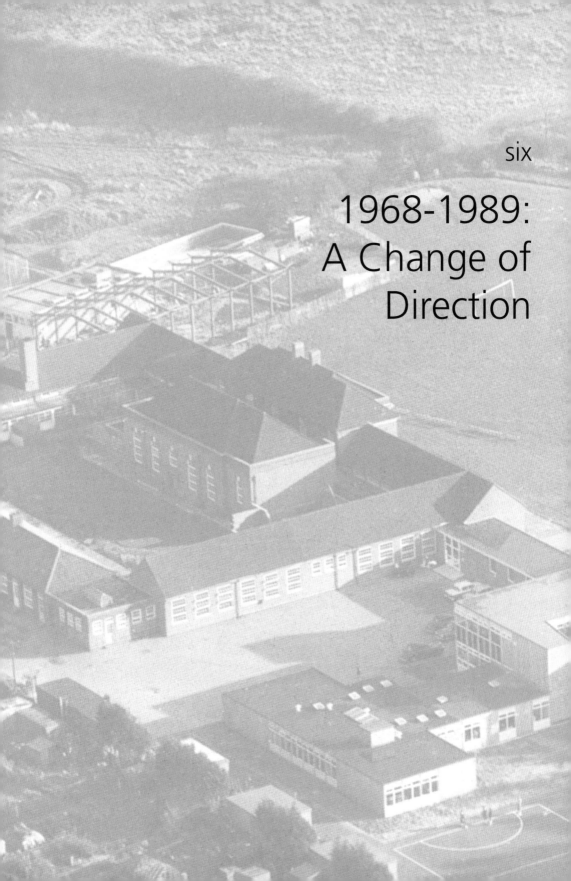

six

1968-1989:
A Change of
Direction

During the 1960s many new schools were built in Essex and others were enlarged to cope with increasing pupil rolls. Billericay was one of the first Essex schools to become a comprehensive. Mr Arthur Lingard was appointed headteacher. He arrived in Billericay nine months before the changeover and the school officially became comprehensive on 1 September 1968. The intake of pupils that year was 270, making a total of 670, and numbers steadily expanded until by 1972 the school roll had grown to 1,300. A tremendous building programme, began which upgraded A Block.

Mr Alan Vann, current Deputy Head, remembers the enormous expansion of the school roll during 1972, the year of his appointment. This was also the year when the school leaving age was raised to sixteen. An intake of 300 pupils was not unusual. The Sixth Form began to grow rapidly, becoming one of the largest in Essex.

New buildings in Phase I included a gymnasium, Music department, library and medical room. Phase II incorporated the Science Block C and administration facilities, followed by Creative Arts Block E and the sports hall. Finally, came the fine new F Block for Business Studies and Technology, which was eventually completed in 1988.

Headteacher Arthur Lingard, staff and some pupils of Upper School in one of the first photographs taken in the year following the great change to comprehensive education. John Goldwin, who had been headteacher since September 1955, became Head of Lower School and many new teachers were appointed that year. In the fourth year of the new school, there were six students who left to take Honours degrees.

This view shows just how much of the playing field area the pupils took for granted way back in the 1960s before buildings were erected to cater for larger numbers of pupils. The greensward directly in front of the school served as a perfectly flat cricket pitch.

Many of the old classrooms were demolished as each stage of the new building programme was completed, including the air-raid shelters that had later been used as storage sheds. Building continued in various parts of the school for the next twenty years. A bypass road was literally built through the school grounds. This caused tremendous upheaval at the time.

Many pupils at Billericay School were members of the Air Training Corps, which started at the Great Burstead School in 1941. In 1960, former Science teacher and school governor Reg Ferriss formed the Detached Flight of 2243 (Laindon & Basildon) Squadron, which became 2393 (Billericay) in 1962. He is pictured with his cadets in the summer of 1969 when his squadron visited RAF St Mawgan in Cornwall.

It was known that the school was built on the site of Iron Age and Roman settlements of first or second-century occupation. When, in 1970, plans to redevelop the school were proposed, a programme of archaeological excavation and recording was undertaken jointly by the Billericay Archaeological & Historical Society and Essex County Council's Archaeological Department. The late Mr Sam Weller and the late Mr David Bumpstead established a 'watching brief', and many schoolchildren and their parents helped with the work at weekends and after school.

Above: One of the exciting pieces of
pottery discovered by the
archaeologists during the excavations.
Later coins, brooches and other
interesting artefacts were found.
These can now be seen in museums
in Colchester, Chelmsford and our
own Billericay Cater Museum.

Right: Many of the families of pupils
at the school were members of the
Billericay Historical & Archaeological
Society and were allowed to take part
in the dig in the early 1970s.
Billericay School pupil Paul Molloy
appeared on television's *Magpie*
programme, describing some of the
exciting finds discovered by the
archaeology team.

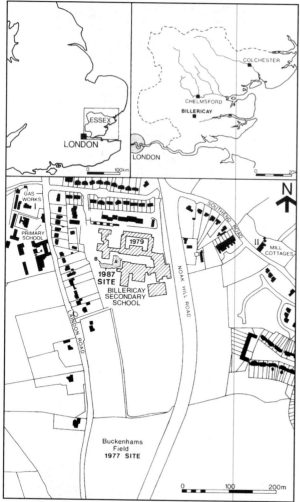

Above: This interesting view (courtesy of Essex County Council) shows the 1987 plan that appeared in the *Essex Archaeology & History Journal*. The aptly named Roman Way, leading to the complex for older people, was built in 1970. A pair of houses, Nos 9 and 11 School Road, were demolished to make way for the new entrance road. The construction of the bypass road in 1973 led to further archaeological work.

Right: This pedestal urn from the first century AD was found during later excavations at Billericay School in advance of further redevelopment work. Staff and pupils helped with the project and it was felt that the work had had an important educational role. (Photograph courtesy of Essex County Council)

Drama has always been a vital part of the school's curriculum. Ray Thomas (centre) was Head of Drama and during the early 1970s he collaborated with Mike Hafferty (left) and Tony Marsden (right), co-directors of Basildon Youth Theatre, to put on excellent productions at the old Towngate Theatre.

Oh, What a Lovely War was a particularly successful performance during 1973. Pictured are Stephen Reeve, Jeremy Patel and Stewart Clark taking a little bayonet practice in readiness for their performance.

Ray Thomas, Head of Drama, was of great inspiration to many students, some of whom went on to perform professionally. One of his productions, *Soap Opera*, received rave reviews when it was performed at the school in 1974. Our picture shows the stars, Stewart Clark and Donna Taylor.

Photographed in 1974, Mr Pat Howard was a much loved teacher, remembered by generations of pupils. Born in Brentwood in 1916, he graduated from London University with a double first in history and philosophy, although he taught Maths and Science at Billericay. He served in the Army during the Second World War and went to West Africa, where, as a member of the Army Educational Corps, he was attached to the Green Howards. After demob in 1946, he returned to Billericay School to teach Maths and Science. Pat was a keen member of Billericay Operatic Society, becoming chairman from 1962 to 1967, and later vice-president. He died in April 1997.

Billericay groups and societies often use the school hall for practice and performances. During the mid-1970s, the hall was used for rehearsal by the Mayflower Corps, a superb band of girl musicians, many attending Billericay School. Founded in 1973, the band achieved considerable world-wide success in its time, winning many trophies.

The Billericay Bandstand event, held on 1 February 1975, was well attended with the then Lord Lieutenant of Essex, Colonel Sir John Ruggles-Brise, and the chairman of Basildon Council, Councillor Ronald Austin, presenting awards.

Comedian and actor Lee Evans was a pupil at Billericay School in the mid-1970s. He is remembered by his class-mates and teachers as an entertaining character even then, and he carried his individual style into show business. Now an actor of Hollywood fame, Lee and his family still live in the town.

During the 1970s, Billericay School organised trips on the BL School ship *Uganda*. This lucky pupil was the 500,000th student to board the ship on 16 July 1976 and received a gift.

The headteacher and some of his staff in 1978. From left to right, back row: Claire Soper (French assistant), Graham Loddor, Jim Redmond, Julian Whybra, Mary McLeod, Joy Pibworth. Front row: Mike Trett (Deputy Head), Barbara Bouchard, Jim Hermiston, Ivan Rushton, Steve Collier, Joy Thompson, Arthur Lingard (headteacher). A few years later, Mike Trett became headteacher at the Brentwood County High School.

As today, rugby was a strong sport at Billericay School during the 1970s. This game in 1978 shows players in a Lower Sixth *vs* Upper Sixth match. In the foreground is Simon Ward; on the ground Ian Butts, with Michael Hall, Chris Blackman and Kevin Saltmarsh.

Above left: The 1978 production of *My Fair Lady* with Neil Sansum as Professor Higgins and Susannah Stubbs as Eliza was a magnificent success.

Above right: Jennifer Molloy and Headteacher Arthur Lingard at Buckingham Palace where Jennifer received her Duke of Edinburgh Award in 1980. The Duke of Edinburgh Award system began in 1956 and the Billericay School students regularly receive Gold Awards.

An unforgettable day in May 1980 for Mr Lingard when he received the Churchill Fellowship Medal from former Prime Minister, Margaret Thatcher, for work on Schools/Industry Education in Billericay and in the USA. This day went down in history as the day the SAS stormed the Iranian Embassy and Mrs Thatcher had to leave the presentation ceremony early.

James Smith, Julian Woolford and Marcus Collings with poet Adrian Mitchell in 1982. Mr Mitchell spent two years as 'writer in residence' at Billericay School. Students enjoyed the opportunity of working not only with this talented poet, but also with the then Poet Laureate, Ted Hughes. Roger McGough, Alan Brownjohn, Brian Patten, Fleur Adcock and many other eminent poets also visited. Adrian Mitchell's book *Nothingmas Day* was dedicated to: 'the astonishing children and teachers of Billericay School in Essex where I spent two years as Visiting Writer and where I wrote several of these poems in classrooms when I should have been working'.

Tim Cunningham with his class in 1982. Tim taught English at the school from 1976 to 1996 and inspired many young writers and poets. His first book of poetry, entitled *Don Marcelino's Daughter*, was published by Peterloo Poets in 2001. He has appeared at the Essex Book and Poetry Festivals and has read his work at major events in England and Ireland.

Mary Snowden became Head of Rural and Environmental Sciences in 1978. The original unit was set up by Terry Illsley around 1959. When he left to lecture at Writtle College, Jean Loveday continued and expanded the farm over the next few years before moving to Diss in Norfolk. Mrs Mary Snowden was Head of Rural Sciences from 1978 to 1986, when Stuart Broomhead took over. The first stockman was John Fairweather, followed by Adam Henderson from 1984. Pictured is a contemporary photograph of Mary Snowden with former headteacher Arthur Lingard, Stuart Broomhead and former farm stockman Adam Henderson.

Stuart Broomhead was appointed Head of Rural Sciences in 1986. During its time, the school farm was a very successful enterprise, where many pupils learned the rudiments of farming, growing vegetables and caring for the pigs, cows, sheep and poultry.

Many children will remember the fun of growing their own vegetables in the school's farm gardens. The fresh vegetables were sold to staff and pupils. Several pupils, after training, went on to seek careers in horticulture as a result of their early training at the Billericay School Farm.

Barry Rule and Heather Robinson acted as midwives when stockman Adam Henderson delivered this perky porker and six brothers and sisters on Christmas Day. Adam came to the school farm in 1984. Mandy, the nosiest kid, is keen to get in on the act.

Fred Fulcher, (centre) born in 1920, attended the Great Burstead Board School in 1925 and later entered the Senior Mixed Department, where he was taught by Mr Pat Howard, Mr Cliff Gardam, Mr Frank Martin and Mr E. Wilson Martin, all of whom met up with him in 1984 when he was about to retire from his job as traffic warden.

A memorable day for Mr Lingard and Deputy Chairman of Governors Mr Jack Barren when Billericay School was named as one of the country's finest. Students Anna Bevis and Andrew Westcott are presented with the 1984 Curriculum Award.

School reunions are usually fun. Fred Fulcher, a former pupil, organised four reunion parties at Billericay School from 1987 to 1991 for post-war former pupils. These were held in the school hall and Fred provided the music. Here we see him presenting a cheque for the school charity to Mr Lingard in the newly completed F Block.

Training day for senior staff at Danbury, 1988/89. From left to right, back row: Piers Ranger, Brian Perkins. Middle row: Alan Sims, Jeff Lord, Ivan Rushton, Sue Anderson, Brian Balchin. Front row: Chris Jones, Kate Spiller, Alan Vann, Jo Higgs, Joan Pipe.

On 8 August 1988, pupils and school staff took time from their studies to create this remarkable panorama marking the conclusion of F block, the £1.5 million Business Studies, Craft, Design and Technology building. Another good reason was an early celebration of the school's twenty-first birthday

since becoming a comprehensive. Ron Case, *Evening Echo* photographer, took this spectacular picture. The event, organised by Steven Bownes, Head of PE, was also filmed by John Walker, Head of Media Studies, and was the first school video.

Members of the Modern Languages department, under the direction of Dr Roger Winter, relax at the end of term in 1988. From left to right, back row: Ivan Rushton, Tim Rhodes, Rudi Gotschel. Middle row: Stephanie Gilbert, Gill Gardner, Jenny Harvey, Mary McLeod, Susan Kikkine. Front row: Dr Roger Winter.

When Mr John Stevenson joined the staff in 1987 as the new Head of Music, he brought with him a long and successful association with the International Music Eisteddfod at Llangollen. In 1989, the Billericay Festival Choir competed against many other youth choirs from all over the world and performed exceptionally well. This is now an annual event. The current choir enjoys an enviable musical reputation and has appeared at numerous prestigious venues.

seven

1990s:
A Decade of
New Challenges

Mr Lingard retired at the end of the summer term in 1991, having served twenty-three years as headteacher. In his farewell letter to the parents, he expressed his pride in the high calibre of staff and the tremendous academic success of the scholars. Mr Robert Goodier became headteacher at the start of the autumn term 1991.

By 1991, the Music Studio project was finished and Mr John Stevenson, who followed Mr Stan Hewitt in 1987 as Head of Music, was able to bring a new dimension to the school's musical curriculum. Mr Stevenson, a gifted musician, founded the superb Billericay School Studio Orchestra, complete with rhythm section and singers. They have made many appearances on national television and at prestigious events all over Europe.

The Parents Guild was renamed Friends of Billericay School, and through their efforts over the years, thousands of pounds have been donated for the well-being of the students. Great changes took the school from Local Education Authority to being completely self-governing. The school became one of the largest employers of staff in the town.

Sadly, Mr Goodier retired through ill health in 1997. Mrs Susan Hammond joined the school at Easter 1998 and became the school's first female headteacher, bringing tremendous experience, energy and a brand of management skills that have earned her respect from colleagues and students alike.

This aerial photograph, taken by Dr Roger Winter at the beginning of the 1990s, shows a unique view of the original school built in 1937 (A Block), now surrounded by modern structures to accommodate the needs of pupils.

Non-uniform day is enjoyed by pupils and staff, and also raises money for Children in Need. Here we see teachers Mary McLeod, Janet Cook and Margaret Sturges in the 1991 fund-raiser, dressed in their old school uniforms.

Billericay School achieved great success in the London Weekend Television Arts Festival, held in March 1990, which was televised. Melvyn Bragg presented the prizes. The Billericay School Orchestra, consisting of ten musicians, five singers and six dancers, performed in the ninety-minute showcase for the London TV Arts Festival, alongside other acts selected from the previous heats at the Wembley Conference Centre.

A very proud School Farm stockman, Adam Henderson, with James Woolard, acting as barn dutyman, displaying some of their first prize awards gained at the Essex Show and Young Farmers Club during 1991. They won the Young Farmers Trophy seven years running.

This poster advertised the Final Grand Reunion of old pupils and staff. Fred Fulcher was the organiser and also played drums in the Melodics, his group that had entertained Billericay folk for many years.

The unveiling of the P.G. White memorial plaque. Pictured on the far right is Fred Fulcher, organiser, with Mrs Charles Howard (Mr White's daughter) and members of the committee and pupils.

After twenty-three years as headteacher of Billericay School, Arthur Lingard retired in 1991. Pictured are Mr and Mrs Lingard with School Office Manager Mrs Lin Bell.

Mr Robert Goodier arrives to take up his post as the new headteacher of Billericay School in 1991.

Stuart Broomhead with a group of pupils, Nicola Redman, Hayley Babb, Jodi Taylor, Laura Hannant, Charlotte Cottrell and Laura Irvin, in 1992. Mr Broomhead was then responsible for Rural Sciences at the school farm, but has also, for many years, organised the Duke of Edinburgh Award Scheme, involving many students every year.

A musical gathering in 1992 shows, from left to right: Mrs Joyce Norris, Mrs Judith Whittaker and ninety-nine-year-old Mrs Mabel White, wife of Billericay School's former headteacher, Mr P.G. White. She also taught at the school. Mrs White was one of the founders of the Billericay Operatic Society in 1929 and was musical director for the first production of the *Mikado* that year. Mrs Norris, who took part in that 1929 production, is now president of BOS. Mrs Whittaker was chairman.

During the 1990s, the Billericay Studio Orchestra made six appearances on BBC television's *Blue Peter*. They are seen here on stage with Anthea Turner and John Leslie during an early 1990s edition of *Blue Peter*.

In 1992, after lying derelict for a few years, the old Great Burstead Board School was completely restored. It acquired a new life when the Billericay Arts Association took over the administration of the rear classrooms. Now known as the Fold, it is still a place of learning, but for slightly older folk. One side of the old school was opened as Quilters, which is now a successful restaurant and night club, while more scholarly endeavours take place at the Fold.

Jenny Moore joined the school staff a decade ago. As the school business manager, with an annual budget of more than £6 million, a staff of 100 teachers and as many support staff, a sports hall, catering team and premises covering many acres, her role is vital. Jenny's responsibilities range from dealing with outside contractors to personnel and payroll. Her present position is a far cry from her early days at Billericay School back in 1993.

End-of-term gathering for the Sixth Form in 1994. Brian Balchin is pictured with fellow staff members.

Ian McAllister, former chairman of Ford UK, hands the keys of the new school minibus to Headteacher Robert Goodier in the presence of governors and pupils.

Above: A smiling welcome from Lin Bell, who joined the school as secretary in 1978 and is now the school office manager, with Kathy Doughty, school receptionist since 1987.

Left: Presentation of the third Curriculum Award in April 1997 was made by HRH Princess Anne to Billericay School students Louise Perry and Alex Storey, who are pictured with former Chairman of Governors Peter Owen and Deputy Head Alan Vann.

The opening night of the Globe Theatre on 12 June 1997. A wonderful evening in the presence of the Queen. Head of Drama Elaine Burford is pictured with students Georgie Swan, Kerry Reynolds, Michael O'Rorke, Steven Auvache, Ann-Marie Lytheer, Anne Long and Catherine Moore. A time capsule containing Billericay School artefacts is buried in the foundations of the Globe.

The Duke of Edinburgh Gold Awards Ceremony took place at Chelmsford Cathedral in 1997. This group, with members of other schools, includes Susannah Abrahall, Gita Mackintosh, Laurie Allsopp, Joanne Walker and Louise Perry.

Special needs are a vital part of Billericay School. Around the table are Pam Commons, Hazel Perfect, Jenny Crabb, Sue D'Rozario, Christine Jones, Jackie O'Rourke, Lorraine Seedhouse, Jane Brand and Liz Tinson.

Mrs Sue Hammond arrived at Easter 1998 to become the new headteacher. She is pictured here with Sophie and Chloë Garwood.

Three deputy headteachers pictured in 1998: Mr Alan Vann, Mrs Jo Higgs (who retired in 2002) and Mr Alan Sims.

Mr Jim Macbeth has been teaching at Billericay School since 1979. Now Head of Lower School, six students – Adam Turpin, Stuart Shrubb, Kris Slaven, Debi Harris, Kayley Sims and Emma Taylor – offered encouragement in April 1998 as he prepared for his second London Marathon in April. His first successful London Marathon was completed in 1994 and the second, which took three hours twenty-eight minutes, meant that more than £1,000 sponsorship money was donated to Mencap.

Mrs Hammond with pupils in the newly refurbished quadrangle. Work to complete the project took nine weeks and the Friends of Billericay School contributed £15,000 to the re-vamp.

John Stevenson invited fellow staff members to contribute their vocal skills in making a CD to raise money for Children in Need. This was coupled with a Sixth Form technology project. So successful was the CD, that when snippets were played on local radio, profits were doubled when listeners phoned in their orders.

Above: After extensive work, the new Billericay School swimming pool was re-opened in 1999. Students were now able to enjoy enhanced facilities and the pool was open for local swimming clubs at weekends and during after-school hours.

Right: John Stevenson, Head of Music, was voted Billericay's Number One Citizen for 1998, for his work in creating the superb Billericay School Studio Orchestra and for his encouragement in helping his students achieve outstanding musical success.

The Mayflower Rotary Club of Billericay hosted the first Billericay Young Citizens Awards to honour young people who have worked for others in the community.

Every year, Margaret Turner, Head of History, arranges for a group of history students to visit the First World War battlefields at Ypres in France. Pictured at the War Grave Cemetery are teachers Phil Cass, Phil Parkin and Melba Noguera.

Billericay Cricket Club Under-17s are pictured here after beating Ongar by eight runs to win the Brentwood & District Cricket Club final. From left to right, back row: Luke Dawe, Tom Cuff, Alex Sell, John Walford (captain), Nick Butler, Jamie Went. Front row: Alex Hearne, Peter Griffiths, Gary Hynes, Stuart Hynes, Tom Rees, James Dorrington. Billericay were dismissed for 100 before bowling Ongar out for 92.

In 1999 the splendid new research-based learning centre was opened at Billericay School. The centre is a valuable and widely used part of the school and is in continual use before, during and after school hours.

The Modern Languages team, headed by Dr Roger Winter (seated).

Opposite above: BBC television presenter Kate Humble arrived at the school to invite students to take part in the children's BBC *WebWise* programme. The students pictured with Kate Humble include Nicola Carroll, Michelle Low, Sean Timms and Nick Elmy.

Opposite below: Chairman of Governors Mr Robert Orr with pupils celebrating the opening of the newly refurbished quadrangle.

Overleaf: Poem written by Mr Nithart Grützmacher, member of the Einstein Gymnasium in Reutlingen, Germany, for the 25th anniversary of student exchanges with the Billericay School. The student exchanges continue today.

Twenty-Five Years of Exchange with Billericay School

Although I found it somewhat tricky,
I have rhymed on Billericay,
And although this name is strange,
To us it stands for the exchange,
The idea of which is strong –
No wonder it has lived so long.
Twenty-five tremendous years,
Which is half a lifetime: Cheers!

Twenty-five long years ago
Keil and Lingard met, you know,
Between alcohol and beer
They gave birth to a new idea.
That's why, since, the ones in charge
Have always met and drunk at large.
Twenty-five stupendous years
Which is half a lifetime: Cheers!

Lots of kids from here and Britain
Have filled in forms, have hoped and written
Letters full of fear and pride,
Have had their chance, have seen their tide,
Have travelled all the way to come,
Had transitory dad and mum,
Mixed up their languages in pairs,
Had arguments and sweet affairs,
Experienced foreign people's habits,
Looked after foreign children's habits,
Saw castles, churches, parks and caves,
Had dancing parties, trips and raves,
And on farewell days stood in tears,
Which I think is a good thing: Cheers!

And who do you think has made this work?
It must be the people who don't shirk,
Like Uli – clever, tall and nimble,
Who has become of this a symbol
Right as his charming frequent lodger,
Whose name, with awe, we spell as Roger
Right as, rejoicingly, I say; Dutch fairy –
Longstanding years it has been Mary!
And in the records rings the fame
Of many another splendid name
In twenty-five non-ending years.
Exchange with Billericay (which is half a lifetime): Cheers!

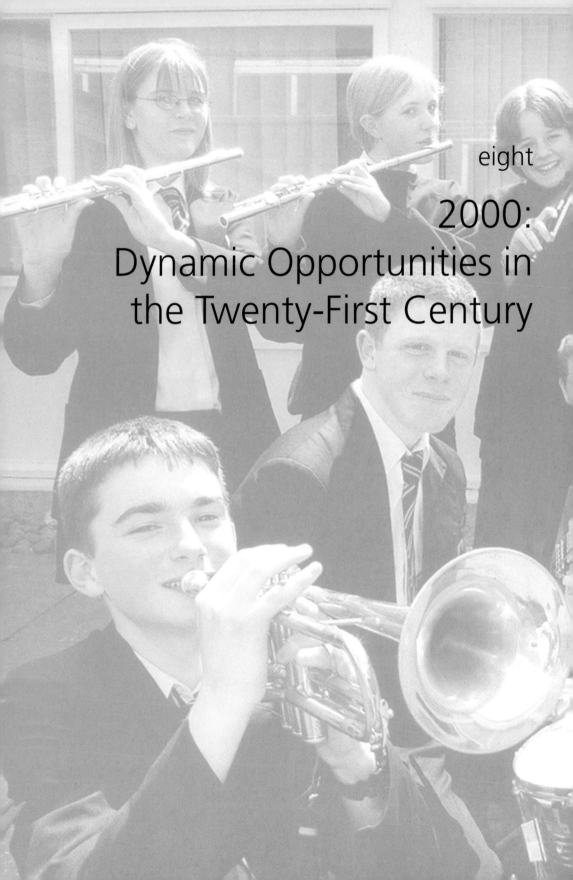

eight

2000:
Dynamic Opportunities in the Twenty-First Century

As part of the Millennium celebrations, Charlotte Spink, Head of Art, and her students created a striking wall frieze to mark the occasion. Postcard-size contributions from all departments were incorporated in the Millennium Wall of Change that still decorates A Block.

The long-awaited Sixth Form Centre was formally opened in May 2000 and is proving to be a great success. It provides a focus for social, academic and study purposes. Sixth Form students come from a wide area, attracted by the variety of courses on offer. The students enjoy outstanding educational resources and the standard of academic excellence is increasing.

In September 2003 the school embarks on an exciting new era as one of the county's first Mathematics and Information Technology Colleges and a Centre of Excellence, collaborating with other schools in the area. Students will now be at the cutting edge of subject areas that will dominate the nation's educational expansion for the foreseeable future. The new finance this status has brought also ensures that its other subject areas will benefit from greater opportunities.

Former Billericay School Headteacher Arthur Lingard, who retired in 1991, joined Headteacher Susan Hammond, Chairman of Governors Robert Orr and students to celebrate the opening of the new Sixth Form Centre in May 2000.

The Billericay School office is perpetually busy. The team that keeps the school running efficiently are, from left to right, back row: Kathy Doughty, Jan Brinkman, Jayne Bradley, Tina Rothery, Lin Bell. Front row: Carol Egelton, Dot Casady, Marianne Went, Linda Chesterton and Margaret Richardson. They dressed up to raise funds for charity.

This successful line-up is the Billericay football team that took part in the School's Cup first-round match against Ernest Bevin School. Back row, from left to right: George Lay, Stephen Lew, Billy Brookes, Wayne Hilditch, Mark Fay, Alan Sexton, Luke Moore, Patrick Flannigan, Jim Flower, Jim Hunter. Front row: Ben Mathers, Matt Russell, Todd Row, Ross Sanders, Sean Quinn, Dean Towey.

Mr Jack Barren served on the governing body of the school for an impressive thirty-nine years. His wife Dorothy marked the first anniversary of his death in February 2000 by presenting a 'Pupil of the Year' award in his memory. The first recipient was Robert Pipe, pictured with Mrs Hammond and Mr Orr.

In May 2000 the Billericay School Studio Orchestra was especially chosen to perform at the Foreign and Commonwealth Office to help celebrate European Day on 9 May – the European embassies and government buildings across London opened their doors for this special occasion.

Elaine Burford's Drama students produced yet another successful performance when Brecht's *The Threepenny Opera* was performed in July 2000. Members of the cast included Robin Norris, Nicholas Gilbert, Mathew James, Stuart Sinclair, Angela Bateman, Matthew Burgess, Robert Hartin, Amy Coppin, Natalea Slessor, Anthony Harvey, Michael Lawn, Anthony Bacon, Adele Lamb, Debbie Harlow, Kierra Marshall, Jaimie McCabe and Jo-Anne Lacey.

In August 2000, the very popular Senior Modern Languages teacher Ivan Rushton retired after thirty-one years.

Charlotte Spink, Head of Art, was delighted when Julian Ellerby, one of her students, won first prize for his design in a competition sponsored by the car design company Sommer Allibert. Introduced during their art classes in 2000, the pupils from Years Seven to Ten worked on the innovative blueprints. Julian in Year Ten won £500 for the school. Also pictured are third-place winner Tara Cross, Charlotte Spink and Jan Dear from Sommer Allibert.

December 2002 saw a visit from the Lord Lieutenant of Essex, Lord Petre (centre), pictured with Mrs Sue Hammond and Chairman of the Governors Robert Orr when he presented achievement awards.

Above: Headteacher Mrs Sue Hammond and three pupils pay their respects at Billericay War Memorial on Armistice Day 2001.

Right: James Dorrington, a very popular pupil at Billericay School, died on 1 January 2002 after fourteen months bravely fighting a brain tumour. Part of the proceeds of this book will be donated to the Children's Ward at Great Ormond Street Hospital in James's memory.

For many years the pupils at Billericay School have taken part in the annual public speaking competitions organised by local Rotarians, competing against other senior schools in the south east. At the March 2002 event, following in the wake of the successful Rotary International Youth Speaks Competition, the school's public speaking group once again brought back many trophies.

As a result of the success of the Friends Reunited website, Billericay School was chosen to be filmed for their March 2002 reunion, organised by Karin Ridgers. The pupils from 1980 to 1987 were filmed by the Christmas Television Company and the programme was shown on Channel Five in May that year. Karin and Clare Baker are pictured handing cheques to representatives of Hamelin House and Little Haven charities.

During the March 2002 reunion, former pupil and editor of the *Enquirer* Carol Driver chats with her former teachers, John Walker and Sue Hooper.

Several successful reunions were held during 2002 and another happy get-together in June was attended by the pupils of 1973-80 and organised by Linda Elmy (née Cook) and Maxine Saltmarsh (née Gillard). Pictured are Andrew Hems, Linda Elmy, Maxine Saltmash, Steven Blaney and their former English teacher, Mrs Linda Hamilton.

The author with a team of VCE students: Caroline Browse, Iain Seedhouse, Neil Probert, Mark Jones, Joseph Philpott and James Carroll. Also pictured is Alan Elkins, Head of Business Faculty and Vocational Co-ordinator, who arranged the visit to a local publishing house. The students undertook initial market research into the feasibility and method of creating this book, in order to complete a unit of work on their Business Planning project.

Mr Ahson Mohammed joined the school staff in September 2002 to become the new deputy headteacher, replacing Mrs Jo Higgs. He is responsible for Keystage 3 pupils and Information Technology.

Billericay MP John Baron paid a visit to the Sixth Form Common Room at Christmas 2002.

Members of the school's superb resource-based learning centre are kept busy before, during and after school hours. Sandra Bailey (library assistant), Jacqui Clare (librarian), Kim Mapp (library assistant), Melba Noguera (RBLC co-ordinator) and Lesley Pike (library assistant) are pictured on Melba's leaving day on 18 December 2002 before she returned to Gibraltar.

The Billericay School Studio Orchestra appeared in March 2003 at the Emmanuel Church for a wonderful evening of music under the direction of John Stevenson, Head of Music. The orchestra was formed in 1989, following a request by students who wished to perform pop music. The Billericay School Studio Orchestra has played in many venues throughout Britain and Europe, delighting audiences with their renditions of popular music from the 1950s to the present day. Their superb performances have raised large amounts for charity and they have made many appearances on national television and at various prestigious events.

Mrs Hammond and her staff are delighted that by September 2003 Billericay School will be designated an Information Technology and Mathematics College. Seen with Specialist School Director John Osborn are Charlotte Caughton, Laurie Perfect, Rebecca Thorogood, Joe Taylor and Jodie Simmons.

The latest reunion for former pupils of Billericay School who left between 1974 and 1978, along with the ever-supporting Friends of Billericay School Committee in fancy dress. Front row: Jenny Emson, Carol Simons, Judy Smith (chairman) and Lesley Pike, with John Matheson and Gerry Woodcroft in second row.